SATYAJIT RAY

LEGENDS AND LEGACIES

THE BIOGRAPHY OF SATYAJIT RAY

RUPA

Published by
Rupa Publications India Pvt. Ltd 2024
7/16, Ansari Road, Daryaganj
New Delhi 110002

Sales centres:
Bengaluru Chennai
Hyderabad Jaipur Kathmandu
Kolkata Mumbai Prayagraj

Copyright © Rupa Publications India Pvt. Ltd 2024

The views and opinions expressed in this book are the authors' own and the facts are as reported by him which have been verified to the extent possible, and the publishers are not in any way liable for the same.

All rights reserved.
No part of this publication may be reproduced, transmitted, or stored in a retrieval system, in any form or by any means, electronic, mechanical, photocopying, recording or otherwise, without the prior permission of the publisher.

P-ISBN: 978-93-6156-935-7
E-ISBN: 978-93-6156-573-1

First impression 2024

10 9 8 7 6 5 4 3 2 1

Printed in India

This book is sold subject to the condition that it shall not, by way of trade or otherwise, be lent, resold, hired out, or otherwise circulated, without the publisher's prior consent, in any form of binding or cover other than that in which it is published.

Contents

Introduction	7
The Birth of a Legend: From Gorpar Road to Global Fame	9
A Young Dreamer: Ray's Artistic Beginnings	13
In the Shadow of Giants: Ray's Formative Years at Shantiniketan	18
From Visualizer to Visionary: The Advertising Years	25
The Birth of a Masterpiece: The Making of Pather Panchali	32
The Apu Trilogy: A Cinematic Evolution	38
Beyond Apu: Diversifying Ray's Cinematic Portfolio	44
Ray's World: A Glimpse into His Personal Life and Philosophy	51
The Writer's Pen: Ray's Contributions to Literature	55
A Man of Many Talents: Ray as a Composer and Illustrator	59
The Global Journey: Ray's Adventures Beyond India	66

Introduction

Hey there, cinema lovers and art aficionados! Have you ever pondered how a boy from Calcutta, with a passion for storytelling and an eye for detail, grew into a legend who transformed Indian cinema? Let me introduce you to Satyajit Ray, a visionary director, composer, illustrator, and a man whose creative genius left an indelible mark on the world.

Imagine growing up in the bustling streets of Calcutta, surrounded by the vibrant sounds of printing presses, the aroma of freshly bound books, and the lively chatter of a family deeply embedded in the cultural and intellectual fabric of Bengal. Ray was the grandson of Upendrakishore Ray, a pioneer in printing technology and a renowned writer and musician.

Ray's fascination with the arts began at a young age. Whether it was sketching in his notebook, observing the intricate processes at the family's printing press, or devouring books from their extensive library, Ray's curiosity knew no bounds. His mother, Suprabha Ray, recognized and nurtured his burgeoning talents, encouraging him to explore the world of literature and art.

As a student at Ballygunge Government High School and later at Presidency College, Calcutta, Ray's intellectual curiosity blossomed. However, it was his time at Santiniketan, Rabindranath Tagore's university, that truly shaped his artistic vision. Under the guidance of masters like Nandalal Bose and Benode Behari Mukherjee, Ray's skills in illustration and design flourished.

In 1943, Ray's journey took a significant turn when he joined D.J. Keymer, a British advertising agency in Calcutta. This period honed his abilities in visual communication and storytelling. Yet, his heart was drawn to cinema, a medium that he believed had the power to capture the complexities of human life. His passion for film was further ignited during a six-month trip to Europe in 1950, where he watched Vittorio De Sica's "Bicycle Thieves." This exposure to Italian neorealism cemented Ray's resolve to create films that were true to Indian life and culture.

Ray's debut film, "Pather Panchali" (1955), marked the beginning of a new era in Indian cinema. Shot on a shoestring budget with an amateur cast and crew, the film's success was a testament to Ray's unwavering vision and dedication. It won the Best Human Document award at the Cannes Film Festival, catapulting Ray to international fame and paving the way for his illustrious career.

Throughout his life, Ray remained a man of many talents. He composed music for his films, created intricate storyboards, and designed book covers that became iconic in their own right. His literary contributions, especially the creation of the beloved detective Feluda, further showcased his storytelling prowess.

Ray's legacy is celebrated not just for his films, but for his holistic approach to art and life. He believed in the power of cinema to reflect the human condition and championed the cause of realism and humanism in his work. His films, characterized by their meticulous detail, subtle narratives, and deep empathy, continue to inspire filmmakers and audiences worldwide.

So, dear explorers of art and culture, take a leaf out of Satyajit Ray's book—stay curious, embrace creativity, and never stop pushing the boundaries of your imagination. Who knows? You might just create the next masterpiece that will captivate the world!

1

The Birth of a Legend: From Gorpar Road to Global Fame

Early Life in Gorpar Road

Satyajit Ray was born on May 2, 1921, in Calcutta (now Kolkata), at 100 Gorpar Road. This house was not just a family home but also housed a printing press, U Ray & Sons, which Ray's grandfather, Upendra Kishore Ray, established. The family's legacy was deeply rooted in the intellectual and cultural fabric of Bengal. Upendra Kishore was a pioneer in half-tone block-making and an illustrious figure in Bengali literature and music, setting a high standard for the Ray family's creative endeavours.

Satyajit Ray, 22 years old, at Santiniketan

Ray's father, Sukumar Ray, was an eminent poet and writer of nonsense literature, whose untimely death in 1923 left a significant void. Despite this, the influence of his father and grandfather's work profoundly shaped Satyajit's early years. He grew up in an environment filled with books, illustrations, and creative expressions, which undoubtedly sowed the seeds of his future artistic pursuits.

Influences and Education

Ray's early education took place in Ballygunge Government High School, where his natural inclinations towards art and literature began to surface. He spent a considerable amount of his childhood at his maternal uncle's house in Bhowanipur, another culturally rich area of Calcutta. His mother, Suprabha Ray, played a pivotal role in nurturing his artistic talents, often reading stories to him and encouraging his creative expressions.

In 1940, Ray graduated from Presidency College, Calcutta, with a degree in economics, although his passion lay elsewhere. His subsequent enrollment at Santiniketan, Rabindranath Tagore's university, marked a turning point in his life. The serene and intellectually stimulating environment at Santiniketan, combined with the influence of Tagore, deeply impacted Ray. Here, he immersed himself in fine arts, learning under the tutelage of stalwarts like Nandalal Bose and Benode Behari Mukherjee, which refined his artistic sensibilities and honed his skills in illustration and design.

Early Career and First Steps into Cinema

> **Fun Fact:**
>
> **Education at Presidency College:** Ray studied economics at Presidency College, Kolkata, before pursuing the arts at Visva-Bharati University at Shantiniketan, founded by Rabindranath Tagore.

After returning to Calcutta in 1943, Ray joined D.J. Keymer, a British advertising agency, as a junior visualizer. Concurrently, he began designing covers and illustrating books for Signet Press, a venture that brought him closer to the literary and cultural milieu of Bengal. His work on the children's edition of "Pather

Panchali" by Bibhutibhushan Bandopadhyay was particularly significant, as it marked his first encounter with the story that would later become his groundbreaking debut film.

In 1947, Ray co-founded the Calcutta Film Society, which allowed him to indulge in his growing interest in cinema. His interactions with prominent film critics and viewing classic films from around the world broadened his cinematic horizons. A pivotal moment came in 1950, during a six-month trip to Europe, where he was profoundly influenced by Vittorio De Sica's "Bicycle Thieves." This exposure to neo-realism cemented his resolve to make films that were true to Indian life and culture.

The Making of Pather Panchali

Returning to India, Ray embarked on a journey fraught with challenges to bring "Pather Panchali" to life. With limited resources and no formal training in filmmaking, Ray faced numerous obstacles, from financial constraints to logistical issues. The film, shot over three years, was a labor of love, involving a largely amateur cast and crew.

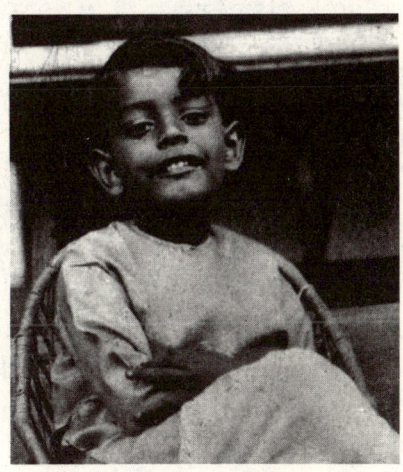

Filmmaker and director Satyajit Ray at his early age

Despite these challenges, "Pather Panchali" premiered in 1955 to critical acclaim, both in India and internationally. The film won the Best Human Document award at the Cannes Film Festival, establishing Ray as a master filmmaker. This success was the beginning of Ray's illustrious career, which included the creation of the iconic Apu Trilogy—"Pather Panchali" (1955), "Aparajito" (1956), and "Apur Sansar" (1959).

Legacy and Global Fame

Ray's films, characterized by their humanism, narrative simplicity, and deep empathy, earned him a place among the greatest filmmakers of all time. His works spanned various genres and included notable films like "Charulata" (1964), "Aranyer Din Ratri" (1970), "Shatranj Ke Khilari" (1977), and "Ghare Baire" (1984). He also made significant contributions to children's literature and illustration, creating beloved characters like Feluda, the detective, and Professor Shonku, the scientist.

> **Fun Facts:**
>
> **Early Career as a Commercial Artist:** Ray began his career in the advertising industry, showcasing his artistic skills by designing book covers and illustrating children's books.

Throughout his career, Ray received numerous accolades, including an honorary Oscar for Lifetime Achievement in 1992, shortly before his death. His legacy continues to inspire filmmakers and artists worldwide, reflecting the timeless and universal appeal of his storytelling.

Satyajit Ray's journey from the narrow lanes of Gorpar Road to global recognition is a testament to his indomitable spirit, creativity, and dedication. His early years, shaped by a rich cultural heritage and personal hardships, laid the foundation for a career that would leave an indelible mark on world cinema.

2

A Young Dreamer: Ray's Artistic Beginnings

Early Environment and Family Influence

Satyajit Ray, affectionately known as Manik, was born on May 2, 1921, in Calcutta (now Kolkata), India. From an early age, Ray was surrounded by a vibrant blend of cultural and intellectual stimuli that would profoundly shape his creative spirit. His family lineage itself was steeped in artistic and literary traditions. His grandfather, Upendrakishore Ray, was a noted writer, painter, and a pioneer in Bengali printing technology. His father, Sukumar Ray, was a celebrated poet, writer, and playwright known for his humorous and satirical works. This rich familial backdrop provided a fertile ground for Ray's burgeoning artistic inclinations.

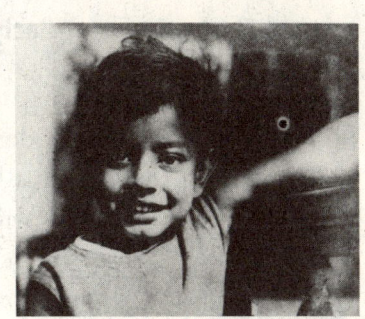

Filmmaker and director Satyajit Ray at his early age

Fascination with Art

Ray's early fascination with art was evident in his childhood. He spent countless hours observing and imitating the artistic activities around him. The family house in Gorpar Road, Calcutta, was not just a home but also housed the printing press, "U. Ray & Sons," where young Satyajit would often watch the intricate processes involved in printing and block-making. This exposure to the mechanics of visual art at such a formative age left an indelible mark on his creative psyche.

As a child, Ray would often be found with a sketchbook, doodling and drawing, a habit encouraged by his mother, Suprabha Ray, who recognized and nurtured his talent. She was his first audience and critic, providing him with the tools and encouragement to explore his artistic interests. Ray's uncle, Subinay Ray, also played a pivotal role in his early artistic development by reviving the children's magazine Sandesh, initially founded by Upendrakishore. Ray contributed illustrations and writings to this magazine, marking the beginning of his artistic journey.

Formal Education and Early Inspirations

Ray's formal education began at Ballygunge Government High School, followed by Presidency College, where he graduated in Economics. However, his heart was always inclined towards the arts. He would often skip classes to visit the Indian Museum and the Calcutta Art Gallery. His visits to these places were not just casual; he meticulously studied the exhibits, particularly the works of Abanindranath Tagore and Nandalal Bose, both stalwarts of the Bengal School of Art. These visits ignited in him a profound

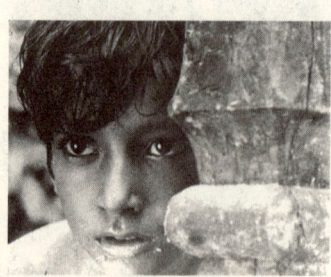

Still from Pather Panchali
Creator: Satyajit Ray, Public domain, via Wikimedia Commons

appreciation for Indian art, which later influenced his cinematic work.

In 1940, Ray joined Rabindranath Tagore's Visva-Bharati University at Santiniketan, where he studied under Nandalal Bose and Benode Behari Mukherjee. The tranquil environment of Santiniketan and the innovative educational philosophy of Tagore provided Ray with a broader perspective on art and life. This period was crucial in shaping his aesthetic sensibilities. The emphasis on traditional Indian art forms and the integration of various artistic disciplines at Santiniketan profoundly influenced Ray's later works.

> **Fun Fact:**
>
> **Directorial Debut with "Pather Panchali":**
> Ray's first film, "Pather Panchali" (1955), gained international acclaim and marked the beginning of the renowned Apu Trilogy.

Influences and Artistic Growth

Ray's time at Santiniketan was transformative. Under the tutelage of Nandalal Bose, he honed his skills in sketching, painting, and design. Bose's emphasis on the importance of Indian art and culture inspired Ray to delve deeper into his heritage. Benode Behari Mukherjee, despite being partially blind, was an exceptional artist and a major influence on Ray. Mukherjee's murals and his approach to art left a lasting impact on Ray, teaching him the importance of detail, observation, and the power of visual storytelling.

During this time, Ray also developed a keen interest in Western art and cinema. He was particularly influenced by the works of the Italian Renaissance masters, whose techniques in chiaroscuro (the use of strong contrasts between light and dark) would later be reflected in his films. His exposure to the world of cinema began with Hollywood films, but it was the discovery of the works of European filmmakers like Jean Renoir and Vittorio De Sica that opened his eyes to the possibilities of filmmaking as a serious art form.

Return to Calcutta and Early Career

Upon returning to Calcutta in 1943, Ray joined D.J. Keymer, a British-run advertising agency, as a junior visualizer. His role involved designing advertisements and book covers, which allowed him to refine his graphic design skills. Ray's work at Keymer was marked by creativity and innovation. He designed the iconic cover for Jim Corbett's "Man-Eaters of Kumaon," which became an instant classic.

Signature of Satyajit Ray

During his stint in advertising, Ray continued his association with Sandesh magazine, contributing illustrations and writings that showcased his growing prowess as an artist and storyteller. His work at Signet Press, where he designed book covers, also brought him in contact with influential literary figures like Bibhutibhushan Bandyopadhyay, whose novel "Pather Panchali" would later become Ray's first film.

Influence of European Cinema

In 1950, Ray embarked on a six-month trip to Europe, a journey that would prove pivotal in his life. He watched 99 films during this period, including Italian neorealist masterpieces like De Sica's "Bicycle Thieves" and Renoir's "The River." These films left a profound impression on him, particularly their naturalistic portrayal of everyday life and their deep humanism. This European sojourn solidified Ray's resolve to become a filmmaker.

Upon his return to India, Ray began working on the script for "Pather Panchali." He drew inspiration from his childhood memories, his artistic training, and the films he had seen in Europe. His meticulous attention to detail, honed through years of sketching and observing, became a hallmark of his cinematic style. Ray's early artistic experiences and his diverse influences coalesced into a unique vision that would soon revolutionize Indian cinema.

Satyajit Ray's artistic beginnings were a confluence of his rich cultural heritage, formal training, and diverse influences. From the vibrant environment of his childhood home to the tranquil artistic retreat of Santiniketan, and the cinematic wonders of Europe, each experience contributed to the making of a visionary artist. Ray's journey from a young dreamer fascinated by art to a master filmmaker was marked by a relentless pursuit of excellence and an unerring dedication to his craft. His early years laid the foundation for a career that would leave an indelible mark on the world of cinema.

> **Fun Fact:**
>
> **Adaptation of Bibhutibhushan's Novel:** "Pather Panchali" was adapted from a novel by Bibhutibhushan Bandopadhyay, demonstrating Ray's talent for blending literature and cinema.

3

In the Shadow of Giants: Ray's Formative Years at Shantiniketan

Introduction to Shantiniketan

In 1940, Satyajit Ray enrolled at Rabindranath Tagore's Visva-Bharati University in Shantiniketan, a place that was destined to become a crucible for his artistic talents and intellectual growth. Shantiniketan, meaning "abode of peace," was founded by Tagore with the vision of creating a space where education and creativity could flourish in harmony with nature. The serene environment, combined with a progressive educational philosophy, made Shantiniketan a unique institution in India.

The Influence of Rabindranath Tagore

Rabindranath Tagore, the Nobel Laureate poet, playwright, and philosopher, was a towering figure whose presence permeated the atmosphere of Shantiniketan. Tagore's emphasis on holistic education, which integrated the arts, humanities, and sciences, profoundly influenced Ray. Tagore's own works, which included poetry, music, and visual art, set a high standard for creative excellence and interdisciplinary exploration. Ray was inspired by Tagore's belief in the power of art to transcend cultural and national boundaries.

Artistic Mentors and Training

Ray's artistic journey at Shantiniketan was significantly shaped by his mentors, Nandalal Bose and Benode Behari Mukherjee, two of India's foremost artists. Nandalal Bose, a disciple of Abanindranath Tagore and a pioneer of the Bengal School of Art, was the principal of Kala Bhavana (the institute of fine arts). Bose's teachings emphasized the importance of traditional Indian art forms and encouraged students to draw inspiration from the country's rich cultural heritage. Under Bose's guidance, Ray honed his skills in drawing, painting, and design, learning to appreciate the subtleties of line, form, and color.

> **Fun Fact:**
>
> **The Apu Trilogy's Global Impact:** The Apu Trilogy, consisting of "Pather Panchali," "Aparajito," and "Apur Sansar," is celebrated as one of cinema's greatest achievements.

Benode Behari Mukherjee, despite his visual impairment, was a master muralist and a profound influence on Ray. Mukherjee's murals, which adorned the walls of Shantiniketan, were characterized by their intricate detail and dynamic compositions. His approach to art, which involved a deep engagement with the subject matter and a meticulous attention to detail, resonated with Ray. Mukherjee's ability to create vivid, expansive works despite his partial blindness taught Ray valuable lessons in perseverance and the importance of inner vision.

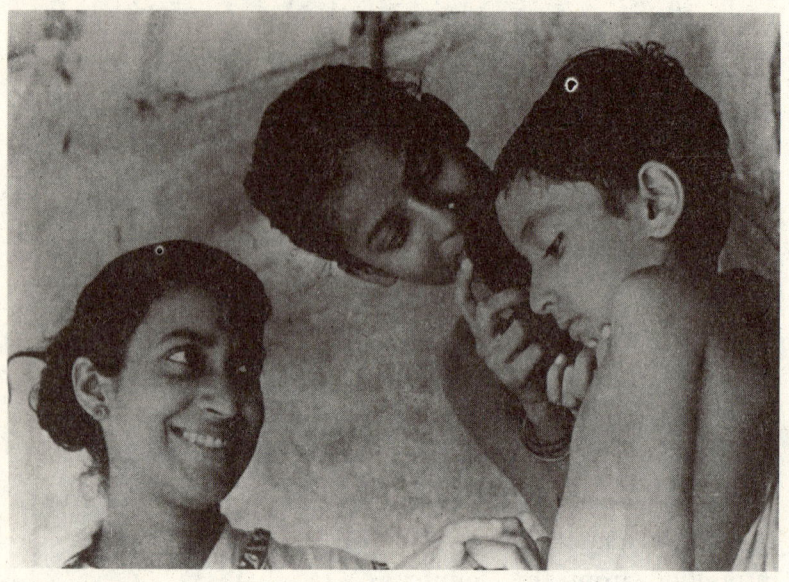

Karuna Bannerjee, Subir Banerjee, and Uma Dasgupta in Pather Panchali.

Interdisciplinary Education and Intellectual Growth

Shantiniketan's curriculum was designed to foster a holistic development, encouraging students to explore various disciplines. Ray's education extended beyond the visual arts to include music, literature, and philosophy. He participated in discussions and debates, attended performances of classical Indian music, and immersed himself in the works of Western classical composers. This interdisciplinary approach broadened Ray's intellectual horizons and deepened his understanding of the interconnectedness of different art forms.

The library at Shantiniketan, with its vast collection of books and manuscripts, became a sanctuary for Ray. He spent countless hours reading works by Indian and Western authors, including Shakespeare, Dostoevsky, and Tagore himself. This voracious reading habit enriched his narrative skills and provided a strong literary foundation for his later work as a filmmaker and writer.

Influence of Nature and Environment

The natural beauty of Shantiniketan, with its lush greenery, open skies, and tranquil ambiance, played a crucial role in Ray's creative development. The integration of nature into the educational experience was a core principle of Tagore's vision. Students were encouraged to observe and draw inspiration from their surroundings, fostering a deep connection with the environment. This immersion in nature not only nurtured Ray's aesthetic sensibilities but also instilled in him a profound respect for the natural world, a theme that would later emerge in his films.

> **Fun Fact:**
>
> **Music Composition for Films:** Ray composed music for many of his films, creating memorable soundtracks that blended Indian classical music with Western influences.

Cultural Exposure and Artistic Freedom

Shantiniketan was a melting pot of cultural exchange, attracting artists, scholars, and students from around the world. This exposure to diverse perspectives and artistic traditions enriched Ray's understanding of global cultures. He interacted with visiting artists and intellectuals, participated in cultural festivals, and observed the performances of traditional and contemporary art forms. This vibrant cultural milieu provided Ray with a broad canvas to experiment and express his creativity without constraints.

Tagore's educational philosophy also emphasized the importance of freedom and self-expression. Students were encouraged to explore their interests and pursue their passions. This freedom allowed Ray to experiment with different mediums and styles, fostering a sense of artistic independence that would define his career.

Personal Growth and Friendships

Ray's years at Shantiniketan were also marked by personal growth and the forging of lifelong friendships. He formed close bonds with fellow students who shared his passion for the arts. These friendships provided a supportive and stimulating environment for creative exchange. Ray's interactions with his peers, who hailed from diverse backgrounds, broadened his social and cultural awareness.

Stamp of India–1994–Scene from Pather Panchali
Credits: Post of India, GODL-India <https://data.gov.in/sites/default/files/ Gazette _Notification_OGDL.pdf>, via Wikimedia Commons

One of Ray's close friends at Shantiniketan was Subhas Mukhopadhyay, who later became a renowned poet. Their shared love for literature and the arts led to many insightful conversations and collaborations. These relationships nurtured Ray's creative spirit and provided a network of like-minded individuals who would later support and influence his work.

Impact on Later Work

The education and experiences Ray gained at Shantiniketan had a lasting impact on his work. The emphasis on traditional Indian art forms, combined with exposure to global artistic trends, helped Ray develop a unique visual style that blended the classical with the contemporary. The interdisciplinary education he received enabled him to infuse his films with a rich tapestry of cultural references and artistic techniques.

> **Fun Fact:**
>
> **"Charulata" and Tagore's Influence:** Ray's film "Charulata" (1964), based on a Rabindranath Tagore novella, showcased his sensitivity to human emotions.

Ray's films often reflect the values and principles he absorbed at Shantiniketan. His deep respect for humanism, empathy for the marginalized, and sensitivity to the nuances of human relationships can be traced back to the philosophical teachings of Tagore and his mentors. The influence of nature and the environment is evident in the lyrical landscapes and evocative settings that characterize his films.

Satyajit Ray's formative years at Shantiniketan were a period of intense artistic and intellectual development. Under the guidance of eminent mentors like Nandalal Bose and Benode Behari Mukherjee, and in the inspiring environment of Tagore's Visva-Bharati University, Ray's artistic skills were honed and his worldview broadened.

Retrospectives and Film Archives: Preserving Ray's Work

The Academy Film Archive in Los Angeles is a key institution dedicated to preserving Satyajit Ray's films. It undertook a comprehensive restoration project to address deterioration and damage, which included digitising the films and enhancing their visual and auditory quality.

The British Film Institute's (BFI) National Archive houses a significant collection of his works and has organised numerous retrospectives and special screenings. These events, featuring discussions and lectures by scholars and critics, have attracted diverse audiences and deepened appreciation for Ray's cinematic legacy.

In the United States, the Museum of Modern Art (MoMA) in New York regularly showcases Ray's films in retrospectives and special screenings. The Berlin International Film Festival, along with other festivals in Tokyo, Paris, Rome, and Toronto, has honoured Ray's legacy through dedicated retrospectives, fostering cross-cultural dialogue and appreciation.

Ray's films are also in curricula, studied for their narrative techniques, visual composition, and thematic depth. Additionally, digital platforms like Criterion Channel, Netflix, and Amazon Prime have expanded access to Ray's work, introducing it to a new generation of cinephiles and ensuring its relevance in the digital age.

4

From Visualizer to Visionary: The Advertising Years

Introduction to the Advertising World

After completing his education at Shantiniketan, Satyajit Ray returned to Calcutta in 1943, where he joined D.J. Keymer, a British-run advertising agency, as a junior visualizer. This marked the beginning of Ray's professional journey in the world of advertising, a period that played a crucial role in shaping his artistic vision and honing his skills in visual storytelling.

Role at D.J. Keymer

At D.J. Keymer, Ray's primary responsibility was to design advertisements, which included creating layouts, illustrations, and visual concepts for various products. His talent for graphic design and his keen eye for detail quickly made him a valuable asset to the agency. Ray's work stood out for its originality and aesthetic appeal, reflecting his ability to blend traditional Indian motifs with modern design elements.

Ray's tenure at D.J. Keymer was not just a job; it was an apprenticeship in the art of visual communication. He learned the importance of clarity and simplicity in design, principles that would later influence his approach to filmmaking. The constraints of advertising—such as the need to convey a message succinctly and effectively—taught Ray how to make every element count, a skill that became evident in the meticulous composition of his films.

Still from the film Aparajito (1956) by Satyajit Ray
Credits: Satyajit Ray Productions/Janus Films, Public domain, via Wikimedia Commons

Work with Signet Press

In addition to his work at D.J. Keymer, Ray began freelancing for Signet Press, a publishing house founded by D.K. Gupta. It was here that Ray's talents found a broader canvas. At Signet Press, he was responsible for designing book covers and illustrating books. This work allowed Ray to exercise greater creative freedom and further develop his distinctive style.

One of Ray's most notable contributions to Signet Press was the design of the cover for Jim Corbett's "Man-Eaters of Kumaon." The cover, with its stark, dramatic depiction of a tiger, became iconic and set a new standard for book design in India. Ray's work at Signet Press was characterized by a deep understanding of the subject matter and an ability to capture the essence of a book through his illustrations and designs.

Growing Interest in Films

While Ray excelled in his advertising career, his passion for films continued to grow. He was an avid moviegoer, frequently visiting Calcutta's cinemas to watch both Indian and international films. His exposure to a wide variety of cinematic styles and genres broadened his understanding of film as an art form. Ray was particularly influenced by the works of European filmmakers like Jean Renoir and Vittorio De Sica, whose films he admired for their humanism and realism.

> **Fun Fact:**
>
> **First Hindi Film "Shatranj Ke Khilari":** In 1967, Ray made his only Hindi film, "Shatranj Ke Khilari," set during British India and highlighting cultural clashes.

Ray's interest in filmmaking was not confined to merely watching films; he began to study them analytically. He dissected the techniques of renowned directors, paying close attention to their use of camera angles, lighting, and narrative structure. This self-taught education in cinema laid the groundwork for Ray's transition from advertising to filmmaking.

The Influence of Jean Renoir

In 1949, Ray had the opportunity to meet the legendary French filmmaker Jean Renoir, who visited Calcutta to shoot his film "The River." Ray assisted Renoir during the production, an experience that proved to be immensely influential. Observing Renoir at work, Ray gained firsthand insights into the art of filmmaking. Renoir's emphasis on naturalism and his empathetic portrayal of characters left a lasting impression on Ray, reinforcing his belief in the power of cinema to reflect the human condition.

Sukumar Ray, children's author and father of Satyajit Ray.

Credits: historytoday.com, Public domain, via Wikimedia Commons

Renoir encouraged Ray to pursue his dream of making films, advice that Ray took to heart. This interaction with Renoir was a turning point in Ray's life, solidifying his resolve to venture into filmmaking. Renoir's influence is evident in Ray's approach to storytelling, characterized by its realism, attention to detail, and deep empathy for his characters.

Establishment of the Calcutta Film Society

Ray's growing passion for cinema led him to co-found the Calcutta Film Society in 1947, along with Chidananda Dasgupta and other film enthusiasts. The society aimed to promote an appreciation for international films and create a platform for cinephiles to discuss and study cinema. The Calcutta Film Society played a pivotal role in Ray's cinematic education,

Fun Fact:

Honorary Oscar for Lifetime Achievement: Ray received an Honorary Oscar in 1992, becoming the first Indian filmmaker to receive this prestigious award.

exposing him to a diverse array of films from around the world.

Through the film society, Ray was introduced to the works of Italian neorealist filmmakers like Roberto Rossellini and Vittorio De Sica, whose films "Rome, Open City" and "Bicycle Thieves" had a profound impact on him. The realism and humanism of these films resonated with Ray, influencing his own cinematic style. The society also provided Ray with access to a community of like-minded individuals who shared his passion for cinema, fostering an environment of intellectual exchange and creative inspiration.

Scriptwriting and the Genesis of Pather Panchali

Inspired by the films he watched and the discussions he participated in at the Calcutta Film Society, Ray began to seriously consider making his own film. He decided to adapt Bibhutibhushan Bandyopadhyay's novel "Pather Panchali," a story that had deeply moved him. Ray saw in the novel an opportunity to depict the beauty and struggles of rural Bengal with a realism that was rare in Indian cinema at the time.

Printed by : Security Printing Press, Nasik

Credits: Post of India, GODL-India <https://data.gov.in/sites/default/files/Gazette_ Notification_ OGDL.pdf>, via Wikimedia Commons

Ray started working on the script for "Pather Panchali" while still employed at D.J. Keymer. His experience in advertising, particularly his ability to convey complex ideas succinctly, helped him in crafting a script that was both evocative and economical. Ray's background in graphic design also influenced his scriptwriting, as he meticulously planned the visual composition of each scene.

Challenges and Determination

Ray's decision to make "Pather Panchali" was fraught with challenges. He had no formal training in filmmaking and limited financial resources. Undeterred, Ray embarked on the project with a small, inexperienced crew and a shoestring budget. His determination and resourcefulness were instrumental in overcoming the numerous obstacles he faced during the production.

Ray's advertising background proved to be an asset in these challenging circumstances. His skills in visual communication and project management enabled him to make the most of the limited resources available. Ray's ability to think creatively and solve problems on the fly was crucial in navigating the logistical and financial difficulties that arose during the making of "Pather Panchali."

Satyajit Ray's years in advertising were a formative period that equipped him with the skills and experiences necessary for his transition to filmmaking. His work at D.J. Keymer and Signet Press honed his abilities in visual storytelling,

> **Fun Fact:**
>
> **Financial Struggles of "Pather Panchali":** Despite its success, "Pather Panchali" faced financial difficulties, with Ray pawning personal belongings to complete the film.

design, and project management, while his involvement with the Calcutta Film Society deepened his understanding of cinema. These experiences, combined with his passion for films and the encouragement from mentors like Jean Renoir, set Ray on the path from being a visualizer to becoming a visionary filmmaker. The journey that began in the advertising world culminated in the creation of "Pather Panchali," a film that would mark the beginning of Ray's illustrious career in cinema and establish him as a master storyteller and a pioneer of Indian cinema.

5

The Birth of a Masterpiece: The Making of Pather Panchali

Introduction to Pather Panchali

"Pather Panchali" (Song of the Little Road) is not just a film; it is a landmark in the history of Indian cinema. Directed by Satyajit Ray, it marks the debut of one of the most influential filmmakers in world cinema. The journey of making "Pather Panchali" was a formidable one, filled with challenges and obstacles. However, it was Ray's unwavering vision and determination that brought this masterpiece to life.

Genesis of the Idea

The idea of adapting "Pather Panchali" into a film came to Ray after he read the novel by Bibhutibhushan Bandyopadhyay. The story, set in rural Bengal, follows the life of Apu and his family, capturing the simplicity and struggles of their existence. Ray was deeply moved by the novel's humanism and realism, and he saw in it an opportunity to depict Indian life in a way that was rarely seen in Indian cinema.

While working at D.J. Keymer and freelancing for Signet Press, Ray began to develop the concept for the film. He wrote the script, staying true to the essence of the novel while incorporating his own artistic vision. His work in advertising and book design helped him conceptualize the visual elements of the film, and his exposure to European cinema provided him with a framework for a realistic and humanistic portrayal of the story.

Pre-Production Challenges

The path to making "Pather Panchali" was fraught with challenges from the very beginning. Ray had no formal training in filmmaking, and his only experience came from observing Jean Renoir during the making of "The River" and from studying films at the Calcutta Film Society. Despite this, Ray was determined to bring his vision to life.

Funding was one of the most significant obstacles Ray faced. He approached several producers and film studios, but none were willing to invest in a film that deviated so drastically from the commercial formulas of Indian cinema. Undeterred, Ray decided to finance the film himself. He used his savings, pawned his wife's jewelry, and took loans from friends and family to gather the initial funds.

> **Fun Fact:**
>
> **Prolific Writer of Children's Literature:** Ray authored popular children's stories, including the detective series featuring Feluda and the scientist Professor Shonku.

Assembling the Crew and Casting

Ray assembled a crew of mostly amateur enthusiasts who shared his passion for the project. Subrata Mitra, who had never worked as a cinematographer before, joined as the director of photography. Ray's background in visual arts and Mitra's keen eye for detail proved to be a perfect combination. Bansi Chandragupta, an experienced art director, took on the role of production designer. Ray's wife, Bijoya, also played an integral role, supporting him through the myriad challenges they faced.

> **Fun Fact:**
>
> **Family Legacy in Arts:**
> The Ray family continues to influence the arts, with his son, Sandip Ray, following in his footsteps as a filmmaker and continuing the Feluda series.

Casting was another hurdle. Ray wanted fresh faces who could bring authenticity to the roles. He chose Subir Banerjee, a young boy with no acting experience, to play Apu. Karuna Banerjee, who had some stage experience, was cast as Sarbajaya, Apu's mother. Chunibala Devi, an 80-year-old retired actress, was persuaded to come out of retirement to play the role of Indir Thakrun, the elderly aunt. The cast, despite their lack of experience, delivered performances that were both natural and poignant.

Filming in Rural Bengal

The decision to shoot on location in rural Bengal added to the film's authenticity but also presented numerous logistical challenges. The village of Boral was chosen for its scenic beauty and its resemblance to the setting described in the novel. The crew had to contend with unpredictable weather, limited resources, and the challenges of working with non-professional actors.

Ray's commitment to realism was evident in his meticulous attention to detail. He insisted on using natural light as much as possible, which led to innovative techniques by Subrata Mitra, such as the use of bounce lighting to achieve the desired effects.

This technique involved reflecting natural light with white bedsheets to illuminate the scenes, creating a soft and realistic look that became a hallmark of the film's visual style.

Financial Struggles and Determination

As the shooting progressed, Ray ran out of funds multiple times. Each time, he had to pause production and seek additional financing. The intermittent nature of the shoot, spread over nearly three years, tested the patience and perseverance of the entire team. Despite these financial setbacks, Ray's determination never wavered. His belief in the project and his vision for the film kept the team motivated through the toughest times.

> **Fun Fact:**
>
> **Designing Film Posters and Titles:** Ray's keen eye for design extended to creating distinctive film posters and credit titles.

Ray's financial struggles caught the attention of the West Bengal government, which eventually provided a grant to complete the film. This support was crucial in allowing Ray to bring his vision to fruition. The government's involvement was not just a financial lifeline but also an endorsement of the cultural significance of the project.

Post-Production and Musical Score

The post-production phase was another critical aspect of the making of "Pather Panchali." Ray's attention to detail extended to the editing process, where he meticulously crafted the narrative to ensure a seamless flow of the story. His background in visual arts and design played a crucial role in the film's editing, allowing him to create a visually coherent and emotionally resonant piece.

The musical score for "Pather Panchali" was composed by Ravi Shankar, one of India's most renowned musicians. Shankar's music, with its haunting melodies and intricate rhythms, perfectly complemented the film's emotional depth and cultural setting. The collaboration between Ray and Shankar resulted in a soundtrack that not only enhanced the film's narrative but also became iconic in its own right.

Still of Subir Banerjee from Pather Panchali.

Credits: Satyajit Ray Productions/Janus Films, Public domain, via Wikimedia Commons

Reception and Impact on Indian Cinema

"Pather Panchali" premiered on May 3, 1955, at the Museum of Modern Art in New York, and later in Calcutta. The film received critical acclaim for its realistic portrayal of rural life, its empathetic storytelling, and its innovative cinematography. It won several awards, including the Best Human Document at the Cannes Film Festival in 1956, bringing international recognition to Ray and Indian cinema.

The impact of "Pather Panchali" on Indian cinema was revolutionary. It broke away from the conventions of mainstream Indian films, which were dominated by melodrama, song-and-dance routines, and star-centric storytelling. Ray's film introduced a new narrative style that focused on the everyday lives and struggles of ordinary people. Its success paved the way for the Indian New Wave, inspiring a generation of filmmakers to explore more realistic and humanistic themes in their work.

THE BIRTH OF A MASTERPIECE

Legacy of Pather Panchali

"Pather Panchali" remains a seminal work in the history of cinema. It established Satyajit Ray as a master storyteller and a visionary director. The film's influence extends beyond Indian cinema; it is considered a classic of world cinema and continues to be studied and admired by filmmakers and critics globally.

The trilogy that followed—"Aparajito" (The Unvanquished) and "Apur Sansar" (The World of Apu)—continued the story of Apu, further cementing Ray's reputation as a filmmaker of extraordinary talent and vision. The Apu Trilogy, with its deep humanism and artistic integrity, stands as a testament to Ray's genius and his contribution to the art of cinema.

The making of "Pather Panchali" is a story of unwavering determination, artistic vision, and the triumph of human spirit against all odds. Satyajit Ray's journey from an advertising professional to a world-renowned filmmaker is an inspiring tale of passion and perseverance. "Pather Panchali" not only revolutionized Indian cinema but also left an indelible mark on world cinema. Its legacy continues to inspire and influence filmmakers, reminding us of the transformative power of art and storytelling.

> **Fun Fact:**
>
> **Fantasy Musical "Goopy Gyne Bagha Byne":** Ray's 1969 film "Goopy Gyne Bagha Byne" became a beloved fantasy musical in Bengali cinema with innovative effects and music.

6

The Apu Trilogy: A Cinematic Evolution

Introduction to the Apu Trilogy

The Apu Trilogy, comprising "Pather Panchali" (1955), "Aparajito" (1956), and "Apur Sansar" (1959), represents a landmark in the history of world cinema. Directed by Satyajit Ray, these three films follow the life of Apu, a boy from a poor Bengali family, as he grows up, faces hardships, and ultimately finds his place in the world. The trilogy is celebrated for its deep humanism, narrative elegance, and innovative cinematic techniques, which together cemented Ray's status as a master filmmaker.

Pather Panchali: The Beginning

"**Pather Panchali**" (Song of the Little Road) is the first film in the trilogy and marks Ray's directorial debut. It tells the story of Apu's childhood in a rural Bengali village. The film's success, both critically and commercially, was unprecedented for an Indian film of its time. It introduced a new form of realism to Indian cinema, focusing on the lives of ordinary people and their struggles.

Cinematic Techniques

Ray's use of natural lighting, location shooting, and non-professional actors brought a raw authenticity to "Pather Panchali." The film's visual style, influenced by Italian neorealism, was groundbreaking. Subrata Mitra, the cinematographer, employed innovative techniques such as bounce lighting, which became a hallmark of the trilogy's visual aesthetic. The sound design, incorporating the natural sounds of the village, and Ravi Shankar's evocative score, further enhanced the film's immersive quality.

Critical Acclaim

"**Pather Panchali**" won numerous international awards, including the Best Human Document at the 1956 Cannes Film Festival. Critics praised its lyrical portrayal of rural life, its empathetic storytelling, and its visual poetry. The film's success brought Ray international recognition and laid the foundation for the subsequent films in the trilogy.

Aparajito: The Unvanquished

"**Aparajito**" (The Unvanquished) continues Apu's story, focusing on his adolescence and the struggles he faces as he moves from his village to the city of Benares (Varanasi) and then to Calcutta for higher education. The film explores themes of family, loss, and the quest for knowledge.

Evolution of Themes

While "Pather Panchali" focused on the simplicity and hardships of rural life, "Aparajito" delves into the complexities of urban life and the challenges of personal growth and education. The film portrays the emotional turmoil of Apu as he navigates his transition from childhood to adulthood, dealing with the loss of his father and later his mother. Ray's nuanced depiction of Apu's evolving relationship with his mother, Sarbajaya, highlights his sensitivity to human emotions and relationships.

Technical and Artistic Growth

Ray's direction in "Aparajito" shows a marked growth in his technical and artistic abilities. The film's cinematography, again by Subrata Mitra, captures the contrasting environments of Benares and Calcutta with a keen eye for detail. The use of light and shadow, the framing of scenes, and the fluid camera movements reflect Ray's increasing command over the medium. Ravi Shankar's music, with its blend of traditional Indian melodies and classical compositions, complements the film's emotional depth.

First Signet Edition of HA JA BA RA LA by Satyajit Ray

Credits: Istikalshah, CC BY-SA 4.0 <https://creativecommons.org/licenses/by-sa/4.0>, via Wikimedia Commons

Reception and Awards

"**Aparajito**" received critical acclaim and won the Golden Lion at the Venice Film Festival in 1957, making Ray the first Indian filmmaker to receive this prestigious award. The film's success solidified Ray's reputation as a visionary director capable of handling complex narratives and deep emotional themes.

Apur Sansar: The World of Apu

"**Apur Sansar**" (The World of Apu) concludes the trilogy, focusing on Apu's adult life, his marriage, fatherhood, and the ultimate acceptance of his responsibilities. The film explores themes of love, loss, and redemption, bringing Apu's journey to a poignant and fulfilling conclusion.

Depth of Characterization

In "Apur Sansar," Ray presents a mature and introspective Apu, played by Soumitra Chatterjee in his debut role. The film's narrative delves into Apu's inner world, his aspirations, and his struggles with the tragedies that befall him. Sharmila Tagore, also making her debut, plays Aparna, Apu's wife, bringing a fresh and naturalistic performance that adds depth to the story.

Innovative Storytelling

Ray's storytelling in "Apur Sansar" is marked by its subtlety and emotional resonance. The film's pacing, the development of its characters, and the intricate interplay of personal and cultural themes demonstrate Ray's mastery over the medium. The cinematography by Subrata Mitra continues to be a strong visual element, capturing the intimacy and expansiveness of Apu's world with equal finesse.

Sukumar Ray and Suprabha Ray, parents of Satyajit Ray (1914)

Credits: Calcutta State Archive, Public domain, via Wikimedia Commons

Critical Reception and Legacy

"**Apur Sansar**" was hailed as a fitting conclusion to the trilogy, praised for its emotional depth and cinematic excellence. The film won several awards, including the National Film Award for Best Feature Film and the Sutherland Trophy at the London Film Festival. The trilogy as a whole is considered one of the greatest achievements in the history of cinema, influencing generations of filmmakers around the world.

Thematic Continuity and Evolution

The Apu Trilogy is celebrated not only for its individual films but also for the thematic continuity and evolution across the three films. Ray's portrayal of Apu's journey from childhood to adulthood is marked by a deep empathy and understanding of human nature. Each film builds on the previous one, creating a rich and layered narrative that explores universal themes of family, identity, and personal growth.

Impact on Indian and World Cinema

The Apu Trilogy had a profound impact on Indian cinema, challenging the conventions of mainstream filmmaking and inspiring a new wave of filmmakers to explore more realistic and humanistic themes. Ray's emphasis on authenticity, his innovative use of cinematic techniques, and his focus on storytelling set a new benchmark for Indian cinema.

> **Fun Fact:**
>
> **Influence of Italian Neorealism:** Ray was influenced by the Italian Neorealist movement and filmmakers like Vittorio De Sica, evident in his early works' social realism.

Internationally, the trilogy established Satyajit Ray as one of the most important filmmakers of the 20th century. Directors like Martin Scorsese, Akira Kurosawa, and Abbas Kiarostami have cited Ray's work as a major influence on their own films. The trilogy's universal themes, combined with its distinctly Indian context, demonstrated the power of cinema to transcend cultural and linguistic boundaries.

The Apu Trilogy represents a cinematic journey that is as much about the evolution of its protagonist, Apu, as it is about the evolution of its creator, Satyajit Ray. Through "Pather Panchali," "Aparajito," and "Apur Sansar," Ray crafted a narrative that is both deeply personal and profoundly universal. The trilogy's success and enduring legacy have cemented Ray's status as a master filmmaker, whose work continues to inspire and resonate with audiences around the world. The Apu Trilogy stands as a testament to the power of cinema to tell stories that are timeless, touching, and transformative.

Poster of Mahanagar

Credits: Ramesh Lalwani, CC BY 2.0 <https:// creativecommons.org/licenses/ by/2.0>, via Wikimedia Commons

7

Beyond Apu: Diversifying Ray's Cinematic Portfolio

Introduction

After the critical and commercial success of the Apu Trilogy, Satyajit Ray continued to explore and expand his cinematic vision. The subsequent years saw Ray diversify his portfolio with a wide range of films that showcased his versatility as a filmmaker. This chapter delves into some of Ray's significant works beyond the Apu Trilogy, including "Charulata" (1964), "The Music Room" (1958), and "The Chess Players" (1977), among others.

Charulata: The Lonely Wife

"**Charulata**," released in 1964, is considered one of Ray's masterpieces. Adapted from Rabindranath Tagore's novella "Nashtanirh," the film tells the story of Charulata, a lonely and intelligent woman in 19th-century Bengal, whose life changes when her husband's cousin, Amal, comes to stay with them.

Thematic Exploration

"Charulata" explores themes of loneliness, intellectual companionship, and unfulfilled desires. The film's protagonist, played by Madhabi Mukherjee, is a complex character whose emotional journey is portrayed with sensitivity and depth. Ray's depiction of Charulata's inner life, her unspoken longing, and the constraints imposed by her social milieu highlight his nuanced understanding of human emotions and relationships.

Cinematic Techniques

Ray's use of visual motifs and symbolism in "Charulata" is masterful. The film's opening sequence, where Charulata moves through her house observing the outside world through opera glasses, sets the tone for her isolated existence. The meticulous set design, costumes, and period details create an authentic portrayal of the time. Subrata Mitra's cinematography captures the intricate emotions of the characters through subtle lighting and composition.

Stamp of India—1994 (Satyajit Ray)

Post of India, GODL-India <https://data.gov.in/sites/default/files/Gazette_Notification_OGDL.pdf>, via Wikimedia Commons

Critical Reception

"**Charulata**" was praised for its lyrical storytelling and visual elegance. It won the Silver Bear for Best Director at the Berlin International Film Festival in 1965 and is often cited by critics as one of Ray's finest works. The film's exploration of female subjectivity and its rich emotional landscape continue to resonate with audiences and scholars alike.

Jalsaghar: The Music Room

"**Jalsaghar**" (The Music Room), released in 1958, is another significant film in Ray's oeuvre. It tells the story of a decadent aristocrat, Biswambhar Roy, who clings to the remnants of his past glory through music and lavish parties, even as his estate falls into ruin.

Themes of Decay and Nostalgia

The film is a poignant exploration of decay, nostalgia, and the passage of time. Chhabi Biswas delivers a powerful performance as the fallen zamindar whose obsession with music and his past leads to his downfall. Ray's portrayal of the crumbling feudal system and the aristocrat's futile attempts to preserve his dignity are both tragic and empathetic.

Visual and Musical Elements

"**Jalsaghar**" is renowned for its visual and musical richness. The grandeur of the music room, with its chandeliers, mirrors, and elaborate decor, contrasts starkly with the dilapidated state of the rest of the mansion. The film's music, composed by Ustad Vilayat Khan, plays a crucial role in conveying the protagonist's emotional states and the film's themes. The classical

Indian performances featured in the film are meticulously choreographed and add to its cultural depth.

Critical Acclaim

"**Jalsaghar**" was critically acclaimed for its atmospheric storytelling and rich symbolism. It is considered a classic in Indian cinema and showcases Ray's ability to blend narrative with visual and musical artistry. The film's exploration of a bygone era and its elegiac tone have made it a timeless piece.

Shatranj Ke Khilari: The Chess Players

"**Shatranj Ke Khilari**" (The Chess Players), released in 1977, is one of Ray's few films in Hindi. Adapted from a short story by Munshi Premchand, the film is set in 1856 on the eve of the British annexation of the Indian kingdom of Awadh. It focuses on two noblemen, Mirza Sajjad Ali and Mir Roshan Ali, who are obsessed with playing chess, oblivious to the political upheaval around them.

Satirical Commentary

The film serves as a satirical commentary on the decadence of the Indian aristocracy and the political complacency that contributed to British colonial dominance. Through the characters of Mirza and Mir, played by Sanjeev Kumar and Saeed Jaffrey, Ray critiques the aristocracy's detachment from reality and their trivial pursuits in the face of looming disaster.

Historical Context and Production Design

"**Shatranj Ke Khilari**" is notable for its historical accuracy and detailed production design. The film meticulously recreates the period's costumes, architecture, and cultural milieu. The nuanced performances, particularly by Amjad Khan as Nawab Wajid Ali Shah and Richard Attenborough as General Outram, add depth to the historical narrative.

Reception and Impact

"**Shatranj Ke Khilari**" received critical acclaim for its incisive social commentary and sophisticated storytelling. It won several national and international awards and is regarded as one of Ray's most ambitious projects. The film's blend of humor, pathos, and political critique exemplifies Ray's versatility and his ability to tackle diverse subjects.

Other Notable Works

Ray's cinematic portfolio beyond the Apu Trilogy includes several other notable films that demonstrate his range as a filmmaker.

Mahanagar: The Big City (1963)

"**Mahanagar**" explores the changing dynamics of a middle-class family in Calcutta when the wife, Arati, takes up a job to support the family financially. The film addresses themes of gender roles, economic pressures, and personal independence. Madhabi Mukherjee's portrayal of Arati is both powerful and nuanced, reflecting the socio-economic realities of the time.

Devi (1960)

"**Devi**" is a haunting exploration of religious fanaticism and the impact of blind faith on a young woman, Doyamoyee, who is believed to be an incarnation of the goddess Kali. Sharmila Tagore's performance as Doyamoyee is compelling, and the film's critique of superstition and patriarchal control is sharp and thought-provoking.

Nayak: The Hero (1966)

"**Nayak**" follows the journey of a matinee idol, Arindam Mukherjee, as he travels by train to receive an award. Through a series of flashbacks and interactions with fellow passengers, the film delves into the complexities of fame, identity, and personal insecurities. Uttam Kumar's portrayal of the protagonist adds depth to this introspective narrative.

Goopy Gyne Bagha Byne (1969)

"**Goopy Gyne Bagha Byne**" is a delightful fantasy adventure film about two village simpletons who receive magical powers from the King of Ghosts. The film's whimsical charm, imaginative storytelling, and musical score by Ray himself made it a favorite among audiences of all ages. It demonstrated Ray's ability to craft engaging stories across genres.

Legacy and Influence

Ray's work beyond the Apu Trilogy solidified his reputation as a master filmmaker with a diverse and rich cinematic portfolio. His ability to explore various themes, genres, and narrative styles showcased his versatility and creativity. Ray's films continue to inspire filmmakers and audiences worldwide, reflecting his deep understanding of human nature and his commitment to cinematic excellence.

> **Fun Fact:**
>
> **Jury Member at Prestigious Festivals:** Ray served as a jury member at major film festivals like Cannes and Berlin, highlighting his global film community status..

Satyajit Ray's post-Apu Trilogy films are a testament to his extraordinary range as a filmmaker. From intimate character studies to grand historical epics, Ray's work covers a vast spectrum of human experience and emotion. His innovative techniques, profound storytelling, and empathetic portrayal of characters have left an indelible mark on world cinema. Ray's legacy as a filmmaker who could seamlessly transition between diverse genres and themes remains unparalleled, cementing his place as one of the greatest auteurs in the history of cinema.

8

Ray's World: A Glimpse into His Personal Life and Philosophy

Early Interest and Philosophy

Satyajit Ray was born on May 2, 1921, into a prominent Bengali family in Calcutta. His grandfather, Upendrakishore Ray, was a writer, painter, violinist, and one of the pioneers of modern block printing. His father, Sukumar Ray, was a celebrated writer of nonsense literature and children's stories, best known for his book "Abol Tabol." This rich cultural and intellectual heritage significantly influenced Ray's artistic sensibilities.

Ray's mother, Suprabha Ray, played a crucial role in his upbringing, nurturing his early interest in the arts. Ray's childhood was marked by frequent visits to the family printing press, where he developed a fascination for visual design and storytelling. His education at Ballygunge Government High School and later at Presidency College laid the academic foundation for his artistic pursuits.

> **Fun Fact:**
>
> **Collaborations with International Filmmakers:** Ray collaborated with international filmmakers and artists, fostering cross-cultural exchanges in the arts.

Personal Life

In 1949, Ray married Bijoya Das, a former actress and singer. Their marriage was a partnership in both personal and professional spheres. Bijoya supported Ray through the various phases of his career, from his initial struggles in filmmaking to his later successes. The couple had a son, Sandip Ray, who followed in his father's footsteps to become a filmmaker.

Ray was known for his towering presence, standing at six feet four inches, and his charismatic yet reserved personality. Despite his fame, Ray led a relatively private life, focusing intensely on his work and his family. He was a voracious reader, an avid music lover, and an accomplished graphic designer. His interests spanned various fields, including chess, calligraphy, and Western classical music, all of which found expression in his films.

Philosophy on Filmmaking

Ray's philosophy on filmmaking was deeply rooted in realism and humanism. He believed in the power of cinema to reflect the human condition and convey profound truths through simple, everyday stories. Ray often quoted the French filmmaker Jean Renoir, who advised him to "look at your own country" for inspiration. This advice resonated with Ray and shaped his approach to storytelling.

Ray's films are characterized by their meticulous attention to detail, subtle narrative style, and deep empathy for the characters. He preferred natural settings and non-professional actors, which lent an authenticity to his films. Ray's visual style was influenced by his background in graphic

> **Fun Fact:**
>
> **Skilled Calligrapher:** Ray's talents included calligraphy, evident in his beautifully handwritten letters and manuscripts

design, evident in his careful composition, use of light and shadow, and the integration of visual motifs.

Ray was also a firm believer in the collaborative nature of filmmaking. He worked closely with his crew, valuing their inputs and fostering a creative environment. Ray's respect for his collaborators and his ability to inspire them contributed to the high quality of his films.

Dedication to the Craft

Ray's dedication to his craft was unparalleled. He was involved in every aspect of filmmaking, from writing the screenplay and designing the sets to composing the music and editing the film. His attention to detail and commitment to excellence set him apart from his contemporaries. Ray's films often took years to complete, reflecting his meticulous approach and unwillingness to compromise on quality.

Satyajit Ray Film at Ajay Nagar, Kolkata

Credits: Pinakpani, CC BY-SA 4.0 <https://creativecommons.org/licenses/by-sa/4.0>, via Wikimedia Commons

Even in the face of financial constraints and health issues, Ray's passion for filmmaking never waned. In the 1980s, after suffering a major heart attack, he continued to make films from his home, dictating scripts and giving directions to his crew. His final film, "Agantuk" (The Stranger), released in 1991, remains a testament to his enduring dedication and creative spirit.

9

The Writer's Pen: Ray's Contributions to Literature

Early Literary Influences

Satyajit Ray's literary journey began long before he made his mark as a filmmaker. Growing up in a family deeply entrenched in the literary arts, Ray was influenced by his grandfather Upendrakishore's children's magazine "Sandesh" and his father Sukumar's whimsical and humorous writings. These early influences shaped Ray's narrative style and his ability to blend humor with profound themes.

Contributions to Sandesh

In 1961, Ray revived "Sandesh," the children's magazine founded by his grandfather, which had ceased publication in 1925. As the editor, Ray infused the magazine with a new vitality, contributing stories, illustrations, and articles that captivated young readers. His contributions were marked by their imaginative storytelling, rich language, and engaging illustrations.

Ray's stories in "Sandesh" often featured young protagonists and adventurous plots, reflecting his understanding of children's perspectives and his ability to craft narratives that were both entertaining and instructive. His illustrations, characterized by their clarity and expressiveness, added a visual dimension to the stories, making them more appealing to readers.

Creation of Feluda

One of Ray's most enduring literary contributions is the creation of the detective character Feluda. Debuting in 1965 in the "Sandesh" magazine, Feluda, whose real name is Pradosh Chandra Mitter, quickly became a beloved figure in Bengali literature. The stories, narrated by Feluda's cousin Tapesh (affectionately called Topshe), follow the detective's adventures in solving complex mysteries.

> **Fun Fact:**
>
> **Documentary on Rabindranath Tagore:** Ray made several documentaries, including one on Rabindranath Tagore, contributing significantly to the understanding of the Nobel laureate's life and works.

Feluda is depicted as a sharp, analytical, and resourceful detective, with a deep knowledge of various subjects and a penchant for disguises. The character's intellectual prowess and moral integrity made him a role model for young readers. Ray's writing in the Feluda series is marked by its crisp prose, intricate plotting, and the seamless integration of cultural and historical references.

The Feluda stories have been adapted into numerous films, television series, and radio dramas, further cementing the character's place in Bengali popular culture. Ray's own film adaptations, such as "Sonar Kella" (The Golden Fortress) and "Joi Baba Felunath" (The Elephant God), brought Feluda to a wider audience and showcased Ray's talent for translating his literary creations into compelling cinematic narratives.

Other Literary Works

Apart from the Feluda series, Ray's literary output includes a wide range of works, from science fiction and fantasy to essays and memoirs. His Professor Shonku series, featuring a quirky scientist and inventor, is another popular creation. These stories blend scientific curiosity with imaginative adventures, reflecting Ray's fascination with science and technology.

> **Fun Fact:**
>
> **Naturalistic Filmmaking Style:** Ray's filmmaking is characterized by simplicity and naturalism, avoiding melodrama to focus on authentic human experiences and emotions.

Ray also wrote several standalone short stories and novellas, many of which explore themes of human nature, societal norms, and the supernatural. His writing is characterized by its clarity, wit, and keen observation of human behavior. Ray's ability to traverse different genres and his skill in storytelling have made him a versatile and respected figure in Bengali literature.

Impact and Legacy

Satyajit Ray's contributions to literature have had a lasting impact on Bengali culture and beyond. His works continue to be read and appreciated by new generations of readers. Ray's ability to engage young minds with his imaginative stories and compelling characters has left an indelible mark on children's literature.

Ray's literary legacy is also evident in the numerous adaptations of his works across various media. The Feluda series, in particular, remains popular, with new adaptations and interpretations keeping the character alive in contemporary culture. Ray's influence on Bengali literature is profound, and his works continue to inspire writers and storytellers.

Satyajit Ray's contributions to literature are as significant as his achievements in cinema. Through his work with "Sandesh," the creation of iconic characters like Feluda and Professor Shonku, and his diverse literary output, Ray demonstrated his prowess as a writer and storyteller. His ability to connect with readers of all ages, his imaginative storytelling, and his dedication to the craft have cemented his place as a literary giant. Ray's literary works, much like his films, are timeless treasures that continue to captivate and inspire.

Ray is credited with pioneering Bengali science fiction through his character Professor Shonku, a scientist who embarks on extraordinary adventures.

> **Fun Fact:**
>
> **Padma Bhushan Award:** In 1978, Ray was awarded the Padma Bhushan, one of India's highest civilian honors, for his contributions to cinema and culture.

10

A Man of Many Talents: Ray as a Composer and Illustrator

Introduction

Satyajit Ray was a polymath whose talents extended far beyond his legendary status as a filmmaker. This chapter delves into Ray's multifaceted abilities as a composer, illustrator, and graphic designer, highlighting the breadth of his artistic contributions and the unique blend of skills that enriched his creative endeavors.

Ray as a Composer

One of Ray's lesser-known yet significant talents was his ability as a composer. His deep appreciation for music was evident throughout his life, and he often integrated his musical sensibilities into his films.

Early Musical Influences

Ray's love for music was nurtured from a young age. Growing up in a culturally rich environment, he was exposed to various forms of music, including classical Western, Indian classical, and popular Bengali music. His father, Sukumar Ray, was a composer and lyricist, and this familial connection to music played a crucial role in shaping Ray's musical inclinations.

Musical Compositions for Films

Ray began composing music for his films with "Teen Kanya" (Three Daughters) in 1961. Over the years, he composed the scores for several of his films, including "Charulata," "Goopy Gyne Bagha Byne," "Aranyer Din Ratri" (Days and Nights in the Forest), and "Shatranj Ke Khilari" (The Chess Players).

> **Fun Fact:**
>
> **Editor of "Sandesh" Magazine:** Ray was an editor and publisher of the children's magazine "Sandesh," originally founded by his grandfather.

Ray's compositions were characterized by their melodic richness and emotional depth. He seamlessly blended Indian classical and folk music with Western musical elements, creating unique soundscapes that enhanced the narrative and emotional impact of his films. For example, in "Charulata," Ray used a mix of Rabindra Sangeet (songs written by Rabindranath Tagore) and original compositions to evoke the cultural milieu and emotional nuances of the story.

Innovative Use of Music

Ray's innovative use of music extended beyond traditional compositions. In "Goopy Gyne Bagha Byne," a fantasy film, Ray created a whimsical and enchanting musical score that complemented the magical elements of the story. The film's songs, with their catchy melodies and playful lyrics, became immensely popular and showcased Ray's versatility as a composer.

Ray's understanding of the role of music in storytelling allowed him to use it not just as an accompaniment but as an integral part of the narrative. His background in Western classical music, combined with his deep knowledge of Indian musical traditions, enabled him to craft scores that were both sophisticated and accessible.

Ray as an Illustrator

Ray's talents as an illustrator were evident from his early years and played a significant role in his career as a filmmaker and writer.

Early Illustrations and Influences

Ray's interest in illustration was nurtured by his family's involvement in the arts. His grandfather, Upendrakishore Ray, was a pioneering illustrator and printer, and his father, Sukumar Ray, was known for his humorous and satirical illustrations. These early influences inspired Ray to develop his own skills as an artist.

Ray's formal training in art at Santiniketan under the guidance of Nandalal Bose and Benode Behari Mukherjee further honed his skills. His exposure to different styles and techniques at Santiniketan enriched his artistic vocabulary and influenced his unique style.

Contributions to Sandesh

As the editor of "Sandesh," Ray contributed numerous illustrations, bringing his stories to life with his expressive and detailed drawings. His illustrations for the magazine were marked by their clarity, humor, and ability to capture the essence of the characters and situations. Ray's work in "Sandesh" showcased his ability to engage young readers visually and narratively.

Book Cover Designs

Ray's talent for illustration extended to book cover designs. During his tenure at Signet Press, Ray designed iconic covers for several books, including Jim Corbett's "Man-Eaters of Kumaon" and Jawaharlal Nehru's "Discovery of India." His designs were noted for their simplicity, elegance, and effectiveness in conveying the essence of the book's content.

Ray's background in graphic design and his understanding of visual composition were evident in his book covers. He used a combination of bold typography, striking images, and thoughtful layouts to create covers that were both aesthetically pleasing and commercially successful.

Storyboard and Film Illustrations

Ray's skills as an illustrator were also integral to his filmmaking process. He meticulously storyboarded his films, creating detailed sketches of each scene. These storyboards served as visual guides during production, helping Ray convey his vision to the cast and crew. His ability to translate his ideas into precise visual representations ensured a high level of coherence and detail in his films.

Rabindranath Tagore 1886

Ray's storyboards are works of art in their own right, showcasing his talent for visual storytelling. They reflect his understanding of composition, perspective, and movement, and highlight his meticulous approach to filmmaking.

Ray as a Graphic Designer

Ray's contributions to graphic design, particularly in the realm of typography and layout, were significant and showcased his innovative approach to visual communication.

Early Work in Advertising

Ray's career in graphic design began with his work at D.J. Keymer, a British-run advertising agency. His role involved creating advertisements, layouts, and illustrations, where he honed his skills in visual communication. His advertising work taught him the importance of clarity, simplicity, and effective messaging, principles that he later applied to his film work.

Design Philosophy

Ray's design philosophy was rooted in the principles of modernism, which emphasized functionality, simplicity, and the use of clean lines and geometric shapes. He was influenced by the Bauhaus movement and the work of designers like Paul Rand and Saul Bass. Ray's designs were characterized by their minimalist aesthetic, balanced compositions, and thoughtful use of typography.

Iconic Film Posters

Ray designed the posters for many of his films, infusing them with his unique artistic sensibilities. His posters for films like "Pather Panchali," "Charulata," and "Goopy Gyne Bagha Byne" are celebrated for their artistic quality and effective communication of the film's themes and tone. Ray's posters were not just promotional tools but works of art that complemented his cinematic vision.

Legacy and Influence

Wes Anderson, Christopher Nolan, and Bernardo Bertolucci have all acknowledged Satyajit Ray's significant influence on their distinctive visual styles and complex narratives, resonating with Ray's exploration of individual and societal dynamics. Ray's influence also extends to younger generations of filmmakers. Contemporary directors like Mira Nair, Ritesh Batra, and Chloé Zhao have all cited Ray as a significant influence on their work. Zhao, who won an Academy Award for "Nomadland," has praised Ray's humanistic approach and his ability to convey the beauty and struggles of ordinary lives.

Ray's legacy is also evident in the numerous retrospectives and film festivals dedicated to his work. Institutions such as the British Film Institute, the Museum of Modern Art in New York, and the Berlin Film Festival have organized extensive retrospectives of Ray's films, celebrating his contributions to global cinema. These events have provided new audiences with the opportunity to experience Ray's work and appreciate its enduring relevance.

> **Fun Fact:**
>
> **Inspiration to Future Filmmakers:** Ray inspired many Indian filmmakers, including Adoor Gopalakrishnan, Shyam Benegal, and Mira Nair.

Influence on Future Generations

Ray's multidisciplinary approach has influenced countless artists and filmmakers. His seamless blending of music, illustration, and design into his storytelling has set a benchmark for integrating various art forms in cinema. Ray's work demonstrates the power of cross-disciplinary creativity and the potential for artists to transcend traditional boundaries.

Recognition and Awards

Ray's talents have been recognized with numerous awards and honors. In 1992, he received an Honorary Academy Award for his lifetime achievements in cinema. His contributions to music, illustration, and design have also been celebrated, with retrospectives and exhibitions showcasing his diverse body of work.

Satyajit Ray was truly a man of many talents, whose contributions to music, illustration, and graphic design have significantly enriched the world of cinema and beyond. His ability to excel in multiple disciplines and integrate them into his filmmaking process set him apart as a unique and visionary artist. Ray's legacy as a composer, illustrator, and graphic designer continues to inspire and influence new generations of artists, affirming his place as one of the most versatile and innovative creative minds of the 20th century.

11

The Global Journey: Ray's Adventures Beyond India

In 1950, Satyajit Ray embarked on a transformative journey to Europe that would profoundly shape his cinematic vision. This trip, spanning six months, was a period of intense exposure to a variety of cinematic styles and storytelling techniques. During his stay in London, Ray watched ninety-nine films, immersing himself in the diverse landscape of European cinema. This period was marked by his deep engagement with the works of Italian neorealists like Vittorio De Sica and Roberto Rossellini, whose films offered a stark, unembellished portrayal of everyday life, emphasizing authenticity and humanism over spectacle. Ray's exposure to these films, particularly De Sica's "Bicycle Thieves," which he saw in London, played a crucial role in shaping his approach to storytelling. He was deeply moved by the film's depiction of poverty and its use of non-professional actors, elements that would later influence his own filmmaking style.

Ray's time in Europe also brought him into contact with French New Wave directors such

> **Fun Fact:**
>
> **Progressive Portrayal of Women:** Ray's films featured nuanced portrayals of women, with characters like Charulata and Arati reflecting his understanding of their inner lives.

as François Truffaut and Jean-Luc Godard, whose innovative narrative techniques and stylistic experiments challenged traditional cinematic norms. This exposure broadened Ray's understanding of the possibilities within the medium of film, inspiring him to push the boundaries of Indian cinema. His diary entries and letters from this period reveal a filmmaker in the making, absorbing influences from all corners of European cinema and contemplating how these techniques could be adapted to tell uniquely Indian stories.

Satyajit Ray with Ravi Sankar recording for Pather Panchali

Moreover, Ray's visit to the British Museum and various art galleries in London enriched his visual sensibility. He studied the works of European masters like Rembrandt and Van Gogh, which honed his appreciation for composition, light, and shadow. These artistic insights would later manifest in the meticulous framing and visual aesthetics of his films. The influence of European art and cinema on Ray was profound, but he was always clear about his goal: to create a cinema that was deeply rooted in Indian culture and experiences while resonating with universal human themes.

Upon his return to India, Ray was determined to translate his European learnings into his debut film. "Pather Panchali," released in 1955, was a testament to this synthesis of Indian narratives with global cinematic techniques. The film's use of natural settings, its focus on the rhythms of rural life, and its empathetic portrayal of its characters drew heavily from the neorealist tradition. However, Ray's unique vision ensured that "Pather Panchali" was not merely an imitation of European cinema but a pioneering work that charted new territory for Indian film. The success of "Pather Panchali" was the beginning of Ray's illustrious career, setting the stage for his emergence as a global cinematic icon.

Ray's European sojourn was not just a period of learning but also of self-discovery.

Cannes Film Festival: The Global Debut

In 1956, Satyajit Ray's debut film, "Pather Panchali," was selected for screening at the prestigious Cannes Film Festival. This marked a significant milestone in Ray's career and the beginning of his international acclaim. The journey to Cannes was fraught with challenges. Financial constraints had plagued the production of "Pather Panchali," with Ray having to secure funding from the West Bengal government to complete the film. Despite these hurdles, the film's inclusion in the festival was a moment of validation for Ray and his team.

> **Fun Fact:**
>
> **Meticulous Planning and Storyboarding:** Ray meticulously planned his films, often sketching scenes and creating detailed storyboards to ensure a clear vision.

"Pather Panchali" premiered to a packed house, with critics and filmmakers from around the world in attendance. The film's reception was overwhelmingly positive, with audiences moved by its lyrical realism and profound humanism. Ray's depiction of rural Bengal, with its attention to detail and deep empathy for its characters, struck a chord with viewers who had never before seen such an authentic portrayal of Indian life on the big screen.

The impact of "Pather Panchali" at Cannes was immediate and far-reaching. The film won the Best Human Document award, a category created specifically to honor its unique contribution to cinema. This recognition catapulted Ray into the international spotlight, garnering him praise from renowned filmmakers and critics. Notable figures like Jean Renoir, who had earlier influenced Ray during his visit to India, and François Truffaut, were effusive in their admiration. Truffaut, in particular, hailed Ray as an exceptional filmmaker whose work transcended cultural and geographical boundaries.

Ray described the festival as a surreal experience, with his film being discussed alongside those of established international directors. The success at Cannes not only validated Ray's artistic vision but also opened doors for future collaborations and screenings at other international festivals.

Satyajit Ray in New York (1981)

Credits: Dinu Alam Newyork, CC BY-SA 4.0 <https://creativecommons.org/licenses/by-sa/4.0>, via Wikimedia Commons

"Pather Panchali" went on to win numerous awards worldwide, including the Kinema Junpo Award in Japan and the Vatican Award in Rome, solidifying Ray's status as a global cinematic icon.

The success of "Pather Panchali" at Cannes had a profound impact on Indian cinema as well. It challenged the prevailing norms of Indian filmmaking, which were largely dominated by formulaic commercial productions. Ray's achievement demonstrated that Indian cinema could produce works of artistic merit that resonated with global audiences. This inspired a new generation of Indian filmmakers to pursue their artistic visions with greater confidence and ambition.

Moreover, the Cannes success underscored the importance of international film festivals as platforms for cultural exchange and dialogue. Ray's work introduced global audiences to the rich tapestry of Indian life and culture, fostering a greater appreciation and understanding of India's cinematic heritage. The impact of "Pather Panchali" at Cannes reverberated through the global film community, paving the way for Ray's subsequent films to be embraced by international audiences and critics alike.

> **Fun Fact:**
>
> **Collaborations with Subrata Mitra and Bansi Chandragupta:** Ray's close-knit team included cinematographer Subrata Mitra and art director Bansi Chandragupta, whose synergy contributed to his films' success.

International Collaborations and Recognitions

Satyajit Ray's success at Cannes was just the beginning of a series of international collaborations and recognitions that would define his illustrious career. His work garnered attention from filmmakers, critics, and audiences worldwide, leading to numerous opportunities for collaboration and accolades from prestigious institutions. One of the most significant collaborations in Ray's career was with the legendary French filmmaker Jean Renoir. Renoir, who visited India in the early 1950s to shoot his film "The River," had a profound influence on Ray. The two filmmakers shared a mutual respect and admiration, and their interactions left an indelible mark on Ray's approach to cinema.

Renoir's influence on Ray was multifaceted. During his stay in India, Renoir encouraged Ray to pursue his own filmmaking ambitions and provided valuable insights into the craft of storytelling and visual composition. Ray's later works, particularly in their emphasis on natural settings and the humanistic portrayal of characters, reflect Renoir's influence. This collaboration was a testament to the power of cross-cultural exchange in the arts, with Renoir's Western sensibilities blending seamlessly with Ray's Indian narrative style.

> **Fun Fact:**
>
> **Retrospectives at Major Film Festivals:** Ray's work was celebrated with retrospectives at international festivals, including the Museum of Modern Art in New York.

As Ray's films gained international acclaim, he was invited to various film festivals and events around the world. His works were celebrated at prestigious festivals such as Venice, Berlin, and Moscow, where they won numerous awards. Ray's films, including "Aparajito" and "Apur Sansar," continued to receive critical acclaim and won major awards, further cementing his status as a global cinematic icon. The recognition from these festivals was not just a personal achievement for Ray but also a significant milestone for Indian cinema, which was increasingly being recognized on the global stage.

Ray's collaborations extended beyond filmmakers to include musicians, writers, and artists from different parts of the world. His association with the British composer Ravi Shankar, who provided the music for "Pather Panchali," is one of the most notable examples. The collaboration between Ray and Shankar brought together two artistic geniuses, resulting in a soundtrack that was integral to the film's emotional resonance. This partnership highlighted Ray's ability to integrate diverse artistic elements into his work, creating a rich, multi-layered cinematic experience.

> **Fun Fact:**
>
> **"Jalsaghar" and the Decline of Aristocracy:** Ray's film "Jalsaghar" (1958), or "The Music Room," poignantly explored the decline of the aristocracy in India.

Another significant collaboration was with the Japanese filmmaker Akira Kurosawa. Kurosawa, known for his powerful storytelling and visual style, was a great admirer of Ray's work. The two artists wrote letters and shared ideas. Kurosawa praised Ray's ability to show how people really feel and what they go through.

Ray's international recognitions were not limited to awards and collaborations. In 1978, he was honored with the prestigious Golden Lion for Lifetime Achievement at the Venice Film Festival, recognizing his outstanding contributions to world cinema. This was followed by numerous honorary doctorates and awards from institutions around the globe, including the Berlin Film Festival, which awarded him the Silver Bear for "Mahanagar" and "Charulata."

The impact of Ray's work on global cinema cannot be overstated. His films were instrumental in shaping the narrative and aesthetic sensibilities of contemporary world cinema. Directors like

> **Fun Fact:**
>
> **Keen Interest in Music:** Ray was not only a filmmaker but also had a keen interest in music, often incorporating his musical knowledge into his films.

Martin Scorsese, Wes Anderson, and Richard Attenborough have cited Ray as a major influence on their work. Scorsese, in particular, has been vocal about how Ray's storytelling techniques and humanistic approach have inspired his own films. These endorsements and recognitions highlight Ray's lasting legacy and his contributions to the global cinematic landscape.

In addition to his collaborations and recognitions, Ray's influence extended to the academic world. His films became subjects of study in film schools and universities across the globe, where they were analyzed for their narrative structure, thematic depth, and visual composition. Ray's approach to filmmaking, characterized by its simplicity and profound humanism, provided valuable lessons for students and scholars of cinema. His masterclasses and lectures at institutions like Harvard and UCLA further solidified his reputation as a thought leader in the field of cinema.

> **Fun Fact:**
>
> **Champion of Social Issues:** Ray's films often addressed social issues, highlighting the struggles and injustices faced by ordinary people.

Hollywood and the Oscar: A Lifetime Achievement

In 1992, Satyajit Ray was awarded the Honorary Oscar for Lifetime Achievement by the Academy of Motion Picture Arts and Sciences.

Ray, who was in frail health at the time, was unable to travel to Los Angeles to receive the award in person. Instead, the Academy arranged for the award to be presented to him in his hospital bed in Kolkata. This gesture was a testament to the respect and admiration Ray commanded within the film industry. The ceremony, held on March 30, 1992, was a moving tribute to Ray's illustrious career. Audrey Hepburn, the iconic actress, presented the award, describing Ray as "one of the greatest filmmakers of our time."

The presentation of the Oscar to Ray was broadcast live, and his acceptance speech, delivered from his hospital bed, was one of the highlights of the ceremony. In his speech, Ray expressed his gratitude to the Academy and his appreciation for the recognition of his work. He reminisced about his early influences, mentioning how seeing De Sica's "Bicycle Thieves" had inspired him to become a filmmaker. Ray's speech was heartfelt and poignant, reflecting his humility and deep love for cinema. His words resonated with audiences worldwide, highlighting the universal appeal of his films and the humanistic values they embodied.

> **Fun Fact:**
>
> **Recognition by the Government of India:** Ray was honored with several awards by the Government of India, including the Bharat Ratna, the country's highest civilian award.

Filmmakers, critics, and fans from around the world celebrated the recognition of a master storyteller whose work had touched countless lives. Martin Scorsese, in a tribute to Ray, remarked that the honor was long overdue and that Ray's films had been a source of inspiration for many filmmakers. Akira Kurosawa, another admirer of Ray's work, expressed his joy at the recognition, stating that Ray's contribution to cinema was unparalleled.

The Oscar ceremony was also a moment of reflection on Ray's vast body of work, which spanned over three decades and included more than thirty feature films, documentaries, and short films. Ray's films, known for their lyrical realism, profound humanism, and deep empathy for their characters, had earned him a place among the greatest filmmakers in history. His works, such as the Apu Trilogy, "Charulata," "Mahanagar," and "The Music Room," were celebrated for their narrative depth, visual beauty, and empathy.

The Honorary Oscar was a fitting recognition of Ray's lifelong dedication to the art of filmmaking. Despite facing numerous challenges, including financial constraints and health issues, Ray remained committed to his vision and continued to create films that were both artistically and socially relevant. His work has left an indelible mark on the world of cinema, influencing generations of filmmakers and captivating audiences with its timeless beauty and universal themes.

> **Fun Fact:**
>
> **Exploration of Human Psychology:** Ray's films delved deep into human psychology, exploring the complexities of human relationships and emotions.

Ray's acceptance of the Oscar also highlighted his deep sense of gratitude towards his collaborators and supporters. In his speech, he acknowledged the contributions of his cast and crew, who had worked tirelessly to bring his visions to life. He also expressed his appreciation for the support of his family, particularly his wife Bijoya, who had been a constant source of strength and inspiration throughout his career.

Ray's receipt of the Honorary Oscar was a moment of triumph, not just for him but for Indian cinema as a whole.

Teaching and Mentorship: Spreading Cinematic Wisdom

One of Ray's most significant contributions to film education was his involvement with the Film and Television Institute of India (FTII) in Pune. Established in 1960, FTII became a leading institution for film education in India, and Ray's association with it brought a new level of prestige and expertise. He regularly visited the institute, delivering lectures, conducting workshops, and providing guidance to students. Ray's interactions with FTII students were transformative, inspiring many of them to pursue their own careers in filmmaking.

In his masterclasses and lectures, Ray emphasized the importance of cultural specificity in storytelling. He believed that films should reflect the unique cultural and social contexts from which they emerged, while also addressing universal human themes. Ray's own films were a testament to this philosophy, combining deeply rooted Indian narratives with universal emotional truths. His teachings encouraged students to explore their own cultural heritage and use it as a foundation for their creative work.

> **Fun Fact:**
>
> **Contribution to Literature:** Ray contributed significantly to Bengali literature with his novels, short stories, and essays, leaving a lasting literary legacy.

Ray also stressed the significance of technical proficiency in filmmaking. He believed that a thorough understanding of the tools and techniques of cinema was essential for effective storytelling. In his workshops, Ray would often demonstrate various aspects of filmmaking, from camera work and lighting to editing and sound design. His practical approach helped demystify the technical aspects of filmmaking, making them accessible to aspiring filmmakers.

One of the hallmarks of Ray's mentorship was his emphasis on storytelling. He believed that a strong narrative was the heart of any good film. Ray's lectures often included detailed analyses of his own films, highlighting the narrative choices and techniques that contributed to their emotional impact. He encouraged students to think critically about their stories, characters, and themes, and to use cinematic techniques to enhance their narrative.

Ray's influence extended beyond India, with his masterclasses and lectures being highly regarded internationally. He was invited to speak at renowned institutions such as Harvard University, the University of California, Los Angeles (UCLA), and the British Film Institute (BFI). These sessions provided a global platform for Ray to share his insights and inspire filmmakers from diverse cultural backgrounds. His teachings were instrumental in promoting a deeper understanding and appreciation of Indian cinema among international audiences.

> **Fun Fact:**
>
> **Founder of the Calcutta Film Society:** Ray co-founded the Calcutta Film Society in 1947, which played a crucial role in promoting world cinema in India.

In addition to his lectures and workshops, Ray's written works also contributed significantly to film education. His books, such as "Our Films, Their Films" and "Speaking of Films," offered valuable insights into his approach to filmmaking and his reflections on the broader cinematic landscape. These writings, rich with Ray's observations and analyses, became essential reading for students and scholars of cinema. They provided a comprehensive understanding of Ray's cinematic philosophy and his contributions to the art of filmmaking.

Ray's mentorship had a lasting impact on the careers of many filmmakers. Directors like Shyam Benegal, Adoor Gopalakrishnan, and Aparna Sen have often cited Ray as a major influence on their work. His guidance and encouragement helped shape their artistic visions and contributed to the development of a vibrant and diverse Indian film industry. Ray's legacy as a mentor is evident in the success and acclaim achieved by these filmmakers, who continue to carry forward his teachings and principles.

Ray's dedication to education and mentorship was driven by his belief in the transformative power of cinema. He saw film as a medium capable of fostering empathy, understanding, and social change. Through his teachings, Ray sought to empower the next generation of filmmakers to use their craft to address important social issues and tell stories that resonated with audiences on a profound level. His commitment to nurturing talent and sharing his knowledge ensured that his influence would endure long after his passing.

> **Fun Fact:**
>
> **Influence on Indian New Wave Cinema:** Ray's work influenced the Indian New Wave cinema movement, inspiring a new generation of filmmakers.

The Legacy Abroad: Influence on Foreign Filmmakers

One of the most prominent admirers of Ray's work is the legendary Japanese filmmaker Akira Kurosawa. Kurosawa, known for his epic storytelling and innovative visual techniques, held Ray in high regard. In numerous interviews, Kurosawa praised Ray's ability to capture the essence of human emotions and experiences with simplicity and elegance. He famously remarked, "Not to have seen the cinema of Ray means existing in the world without seeing the sun or the moon." Kurosawa's admiration for Ray's work is evident in his films, which often reflect a similar focus on the human condition and the subtleties of everyday life.

Martin Scorsese, one of America's most celebrated directors, has also been vocal about Ray's influence on his work. Scorsese has often cited Ray's Apu Trilogy as a major inspiration, praising its narrative depth and visual storytelling. In particular, Scorsese admired Ray's ability to create rich, complex characters and convey their inner lives through subtle visual cues and nuanced performances. Scorsese's own films, known for their character-driven narratives and attention to detail, bear the imprint of Ray's influence. In recognition of Ray's impact on his work, Scorsese played a key role in the restoration and preservation of Ray's films, ensuring that future generations could continue to appreciate his cinematic legacy.

> **Fun Fact:**
>
> **Interdisciplinary Artistic Talent:** Ray's interdisciplinary talents spanned across filmmaking, music, writing, and graphic design, making him a true Renaissance man.

Wes Anderson, the American filmmaker known for his distinctive visual style and quirky narratives, has also acknowledged Ray's influence on his work. Anderson's films, characterized by their meticulous framing, vibrant color palettes, and offbeat characters, often draw comparisons to Ray's visual sensibility. Anderson has spoken about his admiration for Ray's films, particularly "The Music Room" and "Charulata," which he cites as inspirations for their visual composition and narrative elegance. Anderson's appreciation for Ray is evident in his films' attention to detail and the profundity of his characters.

British filmmaker Christopher Nolan, known for his complex narratives and innovative storytelling techniques, has also expressed his admiration for Ray. Nolan has praised Ray's ability to tell compelling stories with simplicity and emotional depth, highlighting the universality of his themes. Nolan's films, which often explore profound philosophical questions and human experiences, reflect Ray's influence in their narrative complexity and emotional connection. Nolan's admiration for Ray underscores the latter's impact on contemporary cinema and his ability to inspire filmmakers across different genres and styles.

Italian filmmaker Bernardo Bertolucci, known for his visually stunning and thematically rich films, was another admirer of Ray's work. Bertolucci's films, such as "The Last Emperor" and "The Conformist," often explore the intersection of personal and political narratives, a theme that resonates with Ray's own explorations of individual and societal dynamics.

Bertolucci praised Ray's ability to weave intricate narratives that reflect the complexities of human relationships and societal structures. His films, characterized by their visual beauty and narrative depth, reflect the influence of Ray's storytelling approach.

> **Fun Fact:**
>
> **Innovative Storytelling Techniques:** Ray employed innovative storytelling techniques in his films, blending traditional narratives with modern cinematic elements.

Ray's influence also extends to younger generations of filmmakers. Contemporary directors like Mira Nair, Ritesh Batra, and Chloé Zhao have all cited Ray as a significant influence on their work. Nair, known for her films that explore Indian and diasporic experiences, has often spoken about the impact of Ray's films on her storytelling. Batra, whose film "The Lunchbox" received international acclaim, has acknowledged Ray's influence in his focus on intimate, character-driven narratives. Zhao, who won an Academy Award for "Nomadland," has praised Ray's humanistic approach and his ability to convey the beauty and struggles of ordinary lives.